YOU THERE!

New & Selected Poems

YOU THERE!

New & Selected Poems

Peter Payack

Zoland Editions

Published by Zoland Editions
Cambridge, Massachusetts
zolandeditions@gmail.com

ISBN: 979-8-218-32315-8

Copyright © 2024 by Peter Payack
www.peterpayack.com

Other Zoland books by Peter Payack:
No Free Will in Tomatoes
Blanket Knowledge

Cover illustration by Mike Payack

Book design by Peter Paul Payack

This book is dedicated to the 117 billion people who have come before me ... and the 117 billion people who will live after me.

A few words about this book and its author
By Roland Pease, Editor and Publisher

I've known poet and conceptual anarchist Peter Payack for nearly half a century. We became good friends from the get-go. I met him on a basketball court (he happened to have a ponytail hanging way down his back) in Cambridge, MA (playing for the Grolier Poetry Book Shop's team, a group Peter had organized) and we instantly connected. Not only was he very friendly, he was unusual in ways I appreciated, serious and funny at the same time, with a very New Jersey bent. He was an individualist I admired, and had all sorts of bright ideas, poetic and philosophical, along with his stellar humor.

When I got to read his quirky poems (published widely in journals including *Rolling Stone, The Paris Review, The New York Times, Asimov's Science Fiction, Samizdat* and *Skunk Piss*), I was taken by them. Over time I ended up publishing two collections of his poetry with my publishing company Zoland Books. And his *No Free Will in Tomatoes* was the first book I published with Z.B.

At Fenway Park, going to hundreds of games together, we shared our new poems, editing them during the innings, rooting the Red Sox along the way.

Linger over these poems. Let yourself think, laugh and be entertained. Go for a ride.

The poems are listed alphabetically. As the editor, I like that way of organizing a poetry book as it provides a randomness I enjoy and respect.

Peter Payack's Poetry
By Phyllis Janowitz, author of Visiting Rites

These are not your usual poems. At a time when most of the poetry to be found these days is going one way – all in the same direction – these poems by Payack are going quite another way. If the other poems are all moving downstream, well then, his are going up.

And this is a good thing, that Payack is writing poems like these. These poems are funny, but these poems are also about big issues. These poems are playful, yet also very serious; they make you think. These are not pretentious poems, these are not pedantic poems, these poems are not ponderous in their "poeticness."

What they are, they are clear, and sharp, and probing, and highly imaginative.

They make one think of the poet, this Peter Payack, as a sort of alchemist, hard at work in his mysterious lair, selecting a bit of this and a bit of that and coming up with something entirely different from what has been made from these bits of this and thats before.

Now, it is a good thing that there is room for all kinds of poetry; but it is a better thing that we have this Peter Payack at work making his poems, these unusual poems, that are hard like mineral elements, at a time when the other poems around these days are maybe from the vegetable or animal kingdom – anyway, they're not coming from the same place. Or maybe they're just not going to the same place.

And when we read a passage such as – "Each evening, shortly after sunset,/ darkness covers the land./ Having mystified thinkers for millennia,/ the mechanism for this occurrence/ has now been identified: migration" (from "The Migration of Darkness") – we enjoy the shock and surprise that comes when we unexpectedly, unpreparedly trip over a thought this fresh and quirky.

How different from what we were expecting! How zany! Yet, how right!

And sometimes that's exactly what a poem should be, should do: take something ordinary, even "poetic" – the darkness and twist it up and turn it around so that 1=2 or A=B, or however these mathematical equations are never supposed to go.

These poems, they do this to the reader time and time again: shock and surprise and make us think. So it's a good thing that Peter Payack is out there, up there in his laboratory; he's inventing these poems at a time when poems like these are not supposed to be invented. Like perpetual motion, or some other law, a rule designed to be broken, which fortunately for us, Payack has gone and broke.

YOU THERE!

New & Selected Poems

ABSOLUTE VALUE AT THE PAWN SHOP

A man with a vision enters the pawn shop with the intended purpose of hocking it for something more substantial, say a pocket watch.

Poor innocent Plato, always trying to relate. And he gives it his best shot, too. In fact, he has the pawn broker listening, telling him his vision is an unchanging eternal idea that has everlasting value and won't diminish with time. He insists the transaction would be an absolute steal: after all, an insight into the ultimate nature of things is surely worth more in ready cash than a pocket watch, especially a used one. What Chutzpah!

But the pawn broker is unconvinced. He is not interested in anything but appearances, as long as he can make a decent living off them.

However, there's something about Plato he likes. He tells him that ever since he saw *Zorba* he's had a soft spot in his heart for all Greeks, even ancient ones. So, risky as it seems, he'll trade something of equal value for Plato's vision.

"How about," the pawn broker suggests, "if I dust off an antique lantern that was hocked some years back by a despairing old cynic named Diogenes?"

Saddened, Plato walks out the door, clinging to his vision.

ANTI-DARWINISM

Survival of the nitwittiest.

ASSEMBLING THE MODEL

A standard model of reality comes to me in the mail. At $4.95 I feel it's quite a bargain. Actually since it's very intricate and made to scale, the kit is worth much more than the money I paid for it. There are three separate bags of different color plastics with an 800-page manual for assembly. The first bag I open is filled with 100 billion galaxies. A small note explains that each galaxy is composed of 100 billion individual stars, an unheard of number of planets, asteroids, and other manifestations of astronomical paraphernalia. Five little jars of paint are supplied with a tiny camel's hair brush to make the stars accurate in appearance. The second bag is filled with philosophical abstracts: Hegelian absolutes, Platonic nouses, and Heisenbergian uncertainties, along with countless thousands of minor conceptions. Some of these are particularly hard for the lay person to grasp, so miniature tweezers are supplied. The third package contains assorted manifestations of things in general: minerals, gravity, human beings, light, artifacts of unknown civilizations, animals, oceans, doubts, food stuffs, inspirations, et cetera. An itemized list, along with a magnifying glass, is included inside the package. I'm very pleased with the model and have it spread throughout the house, ready for assembly. It's not until then that I notice the fine print: "The price of the standard model does not include a tube of glue. The deluxe model of reality ($5.25) contains both a tube of glue and decals."

BLOWING IN THE WIND

I like the idea
of a Buddhist prayer flag

where the vibrations of the wind
blow goodwill and compassion
into the world

while I sit here
strumming Dylan
on my air guitar.

BUG LOVE

Riding along
the Puerto Rican countryside

I notice that each cow
has its very own egret

or to look at it
from another perspective
each egret has its own cow.

One bovine beast
is overheard to mutter:
"Is it true love
or are you just using me
for my bugs?"

To which the egret replies,
"I won't tell you any lies.
I not only love you
but also your flies."

CHERRIES 2016

In the first summer
without my mom

I see black cherries,
her favorites,
at the grocery store.

My heart sinks,
but then soars,
thankful for the memory.

CHRISTO

All wrapped up
in himself.

CONVERSATION

"In the beginning,"
said the father to the wide-eyed son,
"was The Word."

"But before that time,"
asked the curious son,
"would not syllables have existed?"

The father, who had just fallen off his chair,
picked up his pipe, composed himself, and agreed:
*"Ah, yes, um, and before that time
there existed syllables!"*
Seeing the opportunity to again gain
the upper hand, he added,
"And diphthongs."

"But before that time, father,"
inquired the credulous and trusting son,
there surely must have existed solitary letters,
which floated around randomly in the vast vacuum
of infinite space?"

The father,
now pale and perspiring heavily,
consented with a nod
and added,
*"Not only letters, my boy,
but also punctuation marks!"*

By way of summation, the father sternly stated:
"In the beginning was The Word.
Before that time there existed
syllables and diphthongs,
And before that there existed
only solitary letters and punctuation marks,
which floated about randomly and chaotically
in the vast vacuum of infinite space."

Alarmed
at seeing his son's eyes light up
with yet another question,
the father hurriedly pronounced:
"And before that time
the cosmos went unarticulated,
with the exception of occasional
unintelligible
grunts, groans, and belches."

And the father grunted this
with such domineering and unerring authority
that the son fell silent.

CRANIAL CAPACITIES

As of late, some peculiar things have been happening in my head. One day last week I woke up to a symphony orchestra playing Beethoven's *Ninth*. It wasn't the music that disturbed me. Rather it was a lady in the front row who kept complaining about her seat, not being able to see the musicians in the back by the medulla oblongata. Three nights later it was a different matter. There was a blizzard of ideas of bizarre proportions. I certainly would have thought it was a dream if it were not for the snow drifts, which were piled up past my eyelids. I was snowed in for a good part of that day. Then last night, for some reason, Michelangelo decided to paint scenes from Genesis on the ceiling of my skull. When I asked him why he needed the projected four years for its completion, he answered curtly, obviously irritated at my ignorance of such matters. It seems the lighting in my head is poor with little filtering through the openings in my ears.

ECHOES OF THE PAST

Backpacking through the tranquil Maine Woods, my buddies & I stumbled upon something you don't meet up with everyday, an "Echo Lake". When I yodeled a simple "hello" to test it out, you can well imagine how surprised we were to find that this rustic country lake was not only well-educated, but also pretentious enough to show it. It seemed to have taken at least a college level etymology course, because my boisterous salutation ricocheted back first as the Elizabethan "halloa", then the "hallow" of Middle English, followed by the Old French "hallo"! Maybe it attended Harvard Graduate School on a fellowship, because nothing could stop it now. It was as if the echo had been held captive deep in the lake's memory for eons and was only now surfacing and looking for an opportunity to demonstrate its erudition. As the sun started to set, Echo Lake continued reverberating with dimmer yet still decipherable tongues and etymologies passing back through Vulgar Latin, Italic, and even Indo-European variants. This could have been Echo Lake's doctoral defense, so we stood there restlessly, yet respectfully, like a bunch of critical college professors. Throughout that night, even with our heads buried deep in our sleeping bags, we could still hear Neanderthal, Cro-Magnum and Australopithecine phonemes rippling back and forth through the serene stillness. Finally, in the predawn mist, Echo Lake hesitated, yawned, and breathlessly gasped a series of almost inaudible and unintelligible primeval grunts and groans. It only took me and my colleagues a few minutes to groggily confer with one another and award it a "B+" ("A" for effort). After all that, we continued on our hike, carefully lifting our academic robes so as not to stumble over them.

HANGING ON FOR DEAR LIFE

Hanging on for "dear life"
applies across
the whole spectrum of life
from amoebas, trilobites and cockroaches,
to cats, birds and humans.

Life itself,
where a material object
gains a soul,
is precious.

ILLUMINATING THE DARKNESS

Having devoted myself to endless years of abstract study of the abysmal blackness of the Dark Ages, I finally decided to do something pragmatic with all this accumulated knowledge. So I called an electrician who, even though he lacked any precise knowledge of the medieval world, agreed to turn off the electricity, dismantle the outlets, and adapt the existing fixtures to my proposed needs. It was in no time at all before he installed the first illuminated manuscript, *Confessions* by Augustine, into the lamp stand. I then placed a shade on top of it, cutting down the amount of glare and distributing the warm glow to all corners of the room. And some people say that scholarship is non-functional! I placed other manuscripts throughout the house in the expected places. On the night tables in the bedroom I placed matching proofs of "The Existence of God" by Anselm. (I've always prided myself on my interior decorating ability.) The rather ornate but not gaudy Summa Theologica was hung in the dining room above the table. It was a weighty work, so I had to help install it. On top of the refrigerator, where the lamp with the built-in clock used to be, I placed a copy of *A Book of Hours*. I was really pleased with my glowing achievements, until a few nights later when I tripped over myself, as the manuscript in the bathroom burnt out. Luckily, I had a vast library of lesser known and less brilliant manuscripts that I could use as night lights. I replaced the bathroom "bulb" with a loose page from a worm-eaten treatise by a discredited alchemist.

INCREDIBLE CREDO

Even though
I now think of God
as a woman

I still
don't believe
in her/him/them/it.

IT IS TOO HOT

"It is too hot
to live," said
the dead man.

"It is too hot
to be dead," said
the living man.

"It is too hot, let us
not argue," said
the mute man.

"Yes indeed, it is too hot
to waste words on one
another," said the deaf man.

"It is too hot
to write," I said.

"It is too hot
to read the nonsense
you write," she said.

"Fuck you," I said.

"It is too hot," she said.

LEONARDO DA BUG

It is a known fact that among Leonardo da Vinci's illustrious inventions are the chain drive, screwgear & the flywheel. But now it has come to the attention of investigators that a further addition to Leonardo's portfolio has been found. This most striking discovery includes the thoughts, sketches, and a hitherto unknown design of the now ubiquitous cockroach. His first drafts of the mechanism are surprisingly elaborate and technical. They are so close to those in existence today in every detail, that "there is absolutely no doubt as to Leonardo's having invented them", one scholar enthusiastically espoused. Unfortunately, as with Latin and mathematics, Leonardo was ignorant of patent laws, and therefore never received any monetary compensation for his invention. As another scholar so accurately stated, "Why he decided to build such a ghastly creature as a cockroach is anybody's guess. But the thing that troubles me, is that he never got the credit. And it's a damn shame too, because like the light bulb, phonograph & cellphone, the cockroach has become a household item."

LOOPHOLES

In a stunning and unparalleled move, lawyers are beginning to explore an apparent loophole in the long-standing and fundamental law of gravity, in the hopes of overturning it. The lawsuit, which was filed as a class action suit, contends that the law of gravity, by its all-encompassing, one-dimensional nature, is essentially limited in scope particularly in view of our contemporary anything-goes-culture. Antitrust statutes, which severely limit monopolies, will be cited as precedents. If, by means of the courts, lawyers can successfully overturn this centuries-old dictum, it may open vast new possibilities for the restructuring of our society, world, and universe. One practical example would be to utilize ceilings and walls as living spaces and thus alleviate much of the global housing shortage by more than doubling the floor plan of the average dwelling. Not only are lawyers cautiously optimistic about this case, but they are already speculating about their next action: to find a loophole in the second law of thermodynamics, or entropy. According to scientific theory, this classic tenet holds that everything in the material world, including ball point pens, TVs, comets, western civilization, toasters, the ecosystem of the planet, foreign cars, and the very universe itself, is falling apart in an irreversible and unstoppable fashion. "It's about time someone takes this sensitive and delicate matter out of the hands of the bumbling scientists," declared one prominent lawyer and consumer advocate. "Now we'll see," he continues smugly while lifting his eyes skyward, "if we can turn this whole damn mess around!"

METAPHYSICIAN ON CALL

I am amazed that I can fit
the whole Universe
into my head
as I meditate before
falling asleep.

I think of the 100 billion galaxies
    each made up of a 100 billion stars
and the endless, almost bizarre, assortment
of universal fireworks including
    quasars, black holes, shooting stars,
    dark energy, comets, cosmic rays,
    supernovas, meteor showers,
    magnetic storms, exploding galaxies
and the Big Bang.

All this cosmic ruckus
gives me a headache.

I take two aspirin
and resolve to call
a metaphysician
in the morning.

MICHELANGELO & THE CELESTIAL DOME

A wealthy patron of the arts petitioned Michelangelo
    to fresco the firmament
    of the nighttime sky
with "celestial and otherwise cosmic designs."

Up until that time,
    from the beginning of time,
the firmament had been black, stark and dark.
The knowledgeable opinion
was that the cosmos had been hurriedly constructed
    (in less than a week's time
    was the ongoing jest)
with the apparent emphasis on utility and function.
Decorating it, or any esthetic impulses for that matter,
was probably not included in the budgetary allowances.
And the contractor having a celestial dome to build
    with a limited expense account
was understandably hesitant to do any extra work
    no matter how artistic
that wasn't specifically spelled out in the contract.

Michelangelo was at first reluctant
    to accept such a colossal commission
but was cajoled into taking it.
He responded with one of the world's "timeless" masterpieces
bursting with immense power, scope, and vitality.

For this endeavor he constructed a towering scaffold
    upon which he could lie
and paint with the most realistic
and minute detail.

The firmament as envisioned and portrayed by the artist
    is a huge living organism
with billions upon billions of heavenly objects
    majestically and poetically
positioned about the pitch-black dome.

Red giant stars, yellowish moons, planets inhabited by
    peculiar yet intriguing civilizations, galaxies and
    galactic clusters, ringed planets, comets with long
    hairy tails, nebulae, and shooting stars
are all depicted in a most compelling cosmic composition.

He even painted some stars in cunning configurations
    which cleverly suggest such earth objects
    as animals, people, and crafted items.
These designs have come to be known as "constellations".
Wether Michelangelo actually intended the stars
to be perceived in these patterns
as direct representations
or whether they are unintended optical illusions
is a matter of much debate and speculation.

This part of the fresco,
    mainly painted directly overhead,
was completed after four years of back-breaking work.
Yet despite the artist's highly acclaimed accomplishment
    and much to Michelangelo's dismay
he was again called upon to enhance his masterpiece
as his patron demanded something more diverting,
amusing, unearthly, and unimaginable along the edges.

This time, however, much of Michelangelo's displeasure,
    his violent changes in mood, and a sense of being
    at odds with himself, his patron, and the universe
in general became vividly evident in his work.

His previously radiant vision darkened
to include such diabolical and depressing inventions
as an infinite universe forever expanding
    into a cold frozen void of nothingness,
antimatter which annihilates matter upon contact,
exploding galaxies, lifeless bone-dry planets,
    deadly cosmic rays, and black holes
which were depicted as swallowing up and obliterating
much of the masterpiece he had previously painted.

Michelangelo then climbed down from the scaffolding
and stepped back to inspect what his hand had rendered.
    He paused to wonder wearily
if he would be called upon again to aggrandize his work
    with evermore incredible inventions
to meet his patron's insatiable desire
for the fantastic and paradoxical.

MOTORCYCLE EVOLUTION

The size of the human brain
increased from the apelike capacity
of 500 cubic centimeters
in Australopithecus
to about 1500 cc. in modern man.

It took 2 million years
for the human brain to evolve
from the motor size
of a Kawasaki 500
to that of a Harley-Davidson
Super Glide.

NETWORKING FOR DOGS

My dog Maxx (the second x stands for some unknown future disaster for which he will undoubtedly be responsible) starts to bark. He barks for no apparent reason, except that it is 6:30 in the morning. Saturday morning. But now as I strain my ears, I hear a dog in the far off distance, some anonymous animal, barking in somebody else's back yard.

There's probably another dog even farther down the road making that dog bark, like an infinite regress of a mirror reflecting a mirror reflecting a mirror, and so on. That image puts me in mind of the late Argentinean writer Borges' statement that there's something monstrous about mirrors and copulation as they both multiply men. Men! Don't they have dogs in Argentina?

So, my dog is barking, and being the team player that he is, he communicates his message to the next contact, at the appointed time. Somewhere off in the distance, maybe in Argentina, a canine starts this whole cacophonous cycle. What first sounded like my dog barking on the porch, an apparently solitary and annoying act, is really an important part in the worldwide web of dogs.

What the dogs are networking is uncertain.

But one thing I know for sure. It has nothing to do with my getting back to sleep.

NO FREE WILL IN TOMATOES

I place a tomato
on the windowsill
to ripen.

Slowly it turns red.

NO FREE WILL IN TOMATOES II
Quod Erat Demonstradum

My buddy Ron says
"If tomatoes
had free will, Pete,

there wouldn't be
any ketchup."

NO JAMES DEAN
(for Roland on his 50th birthday)

Hey buddy,
at least
you don't have to worry
about dying young
anymore.

PEACE OUT

You cannot out talk
a talker.
You cannot
out scream a screamer.
You cannot
out crazy a crazy person.

PEOPLE PONTIFICATE

All people pontificate
even the Pope.

PERSONALIZED OCEANS

All land animals
are essentially
water inhabiting creatures,
adapted through evolution
to life on dry land.

As humans,
we each carry
a personalized ocean
around with us,
with our consciousness
bobbing up and down
like flotsam
on rolling seas.

POSSIBLE EXPLANATION FOR THE MISUNDERSTANDING

Somehow
after the words
floated from your lips
before reaching my ears

they hung
suspended in space,
momentarily fluttered

and metamorphosed
into a monarch butterfly

only to be caught by
a sudden gust of wind

and carried elsewhere.

REALITY VS THE METAPHORS

A great battle is fought
reminiscent of the Persians and Athenians
on the Plains of Marathon.
A metaphorical force of 100 billion symbols
lands on the shores of reality
and attempts to overtake actuality
with images, allegories, and exaggerations.
It is a harshly fought battle
which spreads throughout the material world
on the besieged fronts of literature.
With an ingenious stroke of military acumen,
the metaphors find both expected and unexpected
similarities in everything literal,
and enslave the world in a vale of illusion.
Everyone drinks from the endless river of Time.
Once-feared Death becomes a long peaceful sleep.
The stars change into grains of sand
only to be blown away by the cosmic wind.
A shadowless blanket of darkness covers the land
as the Sun transmutes into a golden orb
and reality metamorphoses into a poem
by a passionate poet.

RELATIVE RIGHT

Two wrongs
don't make a right
but three lefts do.

RELATIVITY REVISITED

Time only moves
in one direction

except
in your head.

RUMINATING STONEHENGE

Cows graze
in the shadow of Stonehenge.

They don't seem
to notice it.
They don't seem
to notice me.
They don't seem
to notice much of anything.

Whatever might be
the special aura
of Stonehenge,
I don't think
it rubs off on cows.

RUNNING

I hear footsteps
empty as the night
following me.

I run faster and faster
in an attempt to lose them.

They are chasing me.
Matching me step for step.
Following closely on my heels.

It becomes an obsession.
I must beat them,
escape them.

It no longer matters
that they are my own.

SAY WHAT?

She has
all the answers

even when
there are no questions.

SCAVENGER HUNT FOR TRUTH

Instructions:
All things have to be sought after and found by yourself. There is no time limit. Start out by seeking truth in places familiar to you. Leave no stone unturned. Have an open mind.

List: This is what we are searching for:
1. A fig leaf from the garden of Eden.
2. A street map from Atlantis.
3. Diogenes' Lantern.
4. A thread from the fabric of space.
5. The Holy Grail.
6. A stalactite from Plato's Cave.
7. An item bought from the Store of Knowledge.
8. A sample of unpolluted air.
9. One of Demosthenes' pebbles.
10. The chicken who crossed the road.
11. Something laudable from the Delphic Oracle.
12. The ear plugs worn by God at the big bang.
13. A handful of muck from Heraclitus' River of Flux.
14. A photo of Godot or Bardot.
15. A good bit of gossip from the Tower of Babel.
16. Ichabod Crane's travel itinerary.
17. The transcendental state of Nirvana.
18. An iota of military intelligence.
19. A branch from The Tree of Knowledge.
20. Methuselah's Metamucil.
21. A piece of the iceberg that sank the Titanic.
22. A spoke from Apollo's chariot.
23. Sparkling water from the Spring of Life.
24. Manna from Heaven.

25. A nail bent by Thor's hammer.
26. Evidence of intelligent life on Earth.
27. A hair cut by Ockham's razor.
28. A lark from Noah's Ark.
29. The author's luggage last seen on the shuttle to New York.
30. An unthinkable thought.

Send results to:
Aristophanes
"Cloud-cuckoo-land"

SETTING THE MATTER STRAIGHT

"A line that is crooked
in part is crooked in all,
right? Or is it, a crooked
line can never go straight
no matter how many years it
spends in penal institutions?
Or rather, you can't teach a
crooked dog new tricks? Or
maybe it's something about a
crooked man walking a mile
in a back brace for a camel?
I forget exactly how it goes,
but I remember it was by a
Greek philosopher, and when
I read it it made me think:
those ancient Greeks sure
had a way with words."

SNICKERS

Laughter being the best medicine, canned varieties should be stocked on all apothecary shelves. The canned chuckles, which can be used for an endless variety of ailments, might well turn out to be the most economically feasible. They can be stored indefinitely, although if the can is left in direct sunlight for an undue amount of time, the contents might sour. Another likelihood for immediate success is dry wit. This can be kept at room temperature until the doctor prescribes its use. For the more well-read among us, a refined wit might be most appealing. It would undoubtedly be the most expensive, while being effective in a relative limited number of delicate cases. Recent laboratory tests on robotic rats show that this added expense might be unnecessary. From a general point of health, the more roughage (quips, gags, and wisecracks) one ingests, the faster the recovery.

SOMETIMES THE THOUGHTS

Sometimes the thoughts
   in my head
   are so loud
I can't hear the radio playing.

STAR WEB

Gazing at the Milky Way
through the canopy of conifers under which I was camped,
    it seemed to me (in a poetic sense)
that the twinkling web of starlight was attached
to the evergreen needles like a string of blinking bulbs
trimmed on a yuletide tree.

I mused on this until a gust of wind blustered in
    and the gossamer web of stars,
which at first appeared to be affixed gently to the needles,
got downright caught and hopelessly entangled.

This worried me some.

So climbing a nearby tree,
I tried to undo the snarl as best I could.
Unfortunately, being somewhat awkward
    with this delicate sort of thing,
I grabbed hold of the wrong thread, panicked, lost my footing, and
fell out of my tree,
pulling the whole tangled firmament down
around my tent into a hopeless knot.

Talk about mishandling a situation.

Frantically I gathered up the knotted mesh,
    rolled it into a ball,
    dowsed the glow in a bucket of water from a nearby spring,
    and then quietly deposited the stellar evidence
into the campground dumpster.

Luckily for me, dawn was about to break
    when all the stars would vanish anyway.
However, to be on the safe side,
I grabbed my gear and high-tailed it out of camp
    on the off chance I would be found out
    by other campers
who were just then waking.

SURFING AT NIGHT

I had a dream
in which I'm floating
in the 2-billion-year-old ocean
on a bed of blue-green algae.

There was algae as far as I could see,
and I heard a voice say:

"The difference
between living and dying,
being and non-being,
is just where you catch the wave."

I covered my head
with my blanket
and rode the wave back to sleep.

THAR SHE BLOWS
A Cautionary Tale

You do not have
to try to
change the world.

A wayward comet
will do it for you.

THE BARREL & BEYOND

The philosophical pickle ponders both that which is and that which might be beyond The Barrel, as speculative thought is usually described. He wonders what makes a cucumber pickled, and speculates whether life as we know it exists in the Beyond. After many months of study he determines that reality is made up of four primary elements: cucumbers, brine, pickling spices, and The Barrel. Further he concludes that there exists a Prime Mover who not only sets the whole works in motion, but also decides what is to be, gives order to The Barrel and Beyond, and generally operates outside the limits of normal pickle thought and morality. That night, at dinner time, the Prime Mover eats the philosophical pickle with a hamburger.

THE BOW TIE

My buddy Michael (whether or not he should be considered my good buddy I'll let you decide) thought the attire I was planning to wear to the theatre was quite proper. But he suggested I borrow one of his many bow ties to jazz up my appearance a bit. I inspected and rejected a bright red one embossed with miniature cannons for being too loud. A trick one that twirled and squirted water didn't quite achieve the cosmopolitan veneer I was striving for. I simply couldn't find one to fit my personality when Michael got an enigmatic look in his eye. One thing led to another and before I realized it I was being fitted with a bestial ox bow tie. At first I thought it was a bit gauche, the way it hung around my neck, but he assured me it was all very chic indeed! He then lent me a fine leather suit and a snappy pair of snazzy shoes. He also inserted a stylish gold ring in my nose, so I wouldn't get lost in the crowded city streets. Finally, he was kind enough to loan me a small cart, which Michael immediately attached to my ox bow tie, and loaded with my suitcase. Well, enough is enough. But I wasn't familiar with Broadway and these New Yorkers do have an odd way about them. Fortunately for me, once the lights went out and the play started I was no longer concerned about my appearance. And overall, I was very pleased with myself. Not only did I look good, but I minded my manners: I only mooed once or twice, bellowed not at all.

THE CLASSIC EXCUSE

I didn't mean this.
I meant that.

THE ECOLOGIST

The ultimate ecologist is concerned about the amount of energy burned in the shining of the sun while effectively lighting only one half the surface of Earth at a time. He protests by writing three angry letters, noting in each that the 616 million tons of hydrogen used to obtain 612 million tons of helium each second is, to say the least, a bit excessive. He sends them to his senator, his representative, and the Creator of the Universe in care of the local postmaster. One day, a few weeks later, he receives two congenial letters from Washington, thanking him for his interest. That same night, a bolt of lightning strikes his house.

THE END OF THE STORY

"...as she stormed out the door for the final time his jaw dropped like the flap of an old pair of long johns."*

---

* Instead of wasting my summer writing a three-hundred-page novel, I thought I'd just jot down the last line. Maybe you wouldn't have time to read a full novel anyway, being as busy as you are. But please feel free to imagine the rest while you're daydreaming at the beach. If you come up with something really spellbinding (and would fill up at least 299 pages) please feel free to forward it to me in care of my publisher. Be assured I will give you proper credit for your idea, along with a small honorarium, as a token of my gratitude.

THE ETERNAL OPTIMIST

Still waiting for the Comet Kohoutek.

THE EVOLUTIONARY RACE

I run the beach
six miles in two hours,
pathetically slow,
but not bad for a sixty-five year old guy
with two knee replacements.

Then I pass a horseshoe crab
that has gone almost nowhere
in roughly half a billion years.

THE FABRIC OF SPACE

I go into the closet
and pull out my old nightshirt,
Black and full of holes.
I hold it up over my head
and am surprised to find
these holes resemble the stars of the night sky.
I find the constellations Virgo, Orion, and Leo.

There is something paradoxical
about the feel of the fabric.
The areas where there are holes are hot,
while the dark areas are cold
like the deep reaches of interstellar space.
Suddenly, the shirt seems to shrink
before my very eyes!

It is now clear to me
that what I first thought
was a giant moth hole in the middle
is actually a Black Hole
--that theoretical celestial void.
The stars slowly start to move
in a swirling fashion
resembling a galactic spiral.

I drop the nightshirt
as it starts to spin like a fiery pinwheel
on the Fourth of July.
Imploding upon itself
without even so much as a pop,

a nebulous whiff of smoke is
sucked into nothingness.

I'm a little hesitant
about picking out another shirt.

**THE FINE ART
OF COLLECTING ONE'S THOUGHTS**

It isn't every day that one has such a golden opportunity as this: to collect one's thoughts. Seeing that the occasion arose, I decided to spend the whole day at it. I used a 12-foot ladder to collect the most elevated thoughts. After picking these, I placed them, gently, into a wicker basket. Next, I saw that I needed an extra fine net to catch the most fluttering and fleeting of thoughts before they were forever lost to the ozone. I used cheesecloth. Then I borrowed a rake, a shovel, and a pickax to get at those deep, remote thoughts. This was back-breaking work, and took me most of the day. As evening approached, I was lucky to have a strong search lamp in my possession. I used it to hunt out any other rationalizations I could find, no matter how obscure. Paradoxically, they comprised the biggest collection of the lot, as the dim thoughts (thinking the search lamp a light of reason) were attracted to it like moths to a candle.

THE FRUIT RACE

All the armies of the world arm themselves with grapefruit. It is generally agreed that this is a more natural way to wage war. The richer nations stockpile the most, and convert missiles to handle the fruit. Heads of state allocate huge budgets to finance a new generation of bombers especially equipped to handle kilotons of fruit on long-range missions, without spoiling. Soon nations are launching grapefruit, with organically grown guidance systems, into orbit; Russia beats the United States by a week, but the Americans are the first to land a flag-draped grapefruit on the moon. Bigger and better fruits are cultivated to increase striking power and accuracy. One dark day, before a stunned world, the first pineapple-equipped missile is unveiled.

THE GREAT WALL OF WONDER

At the edge of the universe
    there runs a colossal curving wall
beyond which lies an unknowable *nothing*.

Envisioned as a defense barrier
    against this alien void,
the wall was begun in time primeval
    the first foundations being laid
shortly after the big bang.

It's a continuously expanding border,
    which resembles the Great Wall of China
except that its length is measured in light years,
and it is made out of more ethereal materials
including moons, small planets, and asteroids,
    with solidified clouds of cosmic dust
used as celestial cement.

Lofty watchtowers,
with blazing quasars positioned on top,
    were erected at strategic intervals
    to stand on perpetual guard against
the ever-lurking legions of *nothingness*.

THE INFINITE ABYSS

Once mom died
I felt the weight and immensity
of *never* and *forever*.

THE MECHANIC

The cosmic mechanic is an old-fashioned guy
    whose reputation has grown
to all ends of the mechanistic universe.
In addition to standard jobs
    like mufflers, brakes, and shocks,
his expertise includes:
greasing-up spiral galaxies
    to keep them rotating friction free;
tuning-up stars
    to minimize misfiring solar flares
    and eliminate backfiring sun spots;
and balancing & aligning solar systems
    (it's surprising how one unbalanced planet
    can throw a whole system out of whack.)
No ordinary worker is he!

And he's honest, too.
You can trust his personal judgment
as to whether an abused planet
that has been "run to the ground"
    needs a complete overhaul,
or if it is simply time to "junk it"
and invest in a newer model.
He is currently mulling over the fate of Earth.

To show you what a traditionalist he is,
he still provides complete road service
    for a very old-fashioned price.
His most common call for help,
    as you might suspect,

is to come to the aid of cripple comets
which have carelessly wandered too close to the sun.
Most often they have been completely "totaled"
and are unable to move under their own power.
He'll tell it to you straight,
    and then tow the burnt out cinder
to the edge of the observable universe
and push the "heap" over the ultimate edge.

Being a civic minded individual,
    he has erected
(with money out of his own pocket, no less)
a white picket fence on the border of the universe
so that passerbys won't be appalled
    by the discarded wrecks
of planets, stars and galaxies;
their ruined remains rusting and rotting
unceremoniously for all eternity.

Still somewhat of a diehard
    in the field of traditional mechanics,
he won't touch black holes, pulsars or quasars.
He doesn't like to handle these
    "new fangled foreign jobs".
These he leaves in the hands of the younger generation
of newly trained "quantum mechanics"
with their recalibrated tools,
computerized tune-ups,
and relative view of things.

THE METAPHYSICAL EXAM

I was feeling a bit gloomy for a few days
so I made an appointment with my doctor for a check-up.
    Seeing me stumble into his office
with a blank expression, lowered jaw, and drooping shoulders,
he escorted me into his examination room and began with
 the most unusual type of medical procedure:
The Metaphysical Exam.

The first thing he did was to lower the lights
and look deep into the pupils of my no longer twinkling eyes
    with the aid of a small telescope.
He stared with such astonishing intensity that he claimed
to see directly into the innermost essence of my being.
And by the way he was moaning, I was most unnerved.

Next he placed his fingers gently on my wrist
    and felt for the pulse of the infinite.
As my pulse was flashing on and off 30 times a second,
he conceded it might be a trifle rapid.
However, he assured me this was well within the normal range,
especially for a man with my condition.

Then he placed his stethoscope against my chest
    and listened to the rhythms of my heart.
He heard a strong steady beat,
but also some indication of a slight murmur.
This he diagnosed as a faint, agonizing rumble – a remnant
    of the primordial fireball radiation –
he should've been hearing the silences of interstellar spaces.

Finally, he instructed me to stick out my tongue
    and chant *om* in a long drawn-out way.
After several minutes of this,
which frankly felt like an eternity,
the doctor said my tongue and throat looked fine,
    although he was concerned about
the dark patches he saw on my soul.

After he picked me up off the floor,
he told me not to be alarmed as this sickness of the soul
    was something that was going around.
He advised me to elevate my spirits,
    get plenty of rest,
and regularly reach for the stars
to avoid existential bedsores.

THE MIGRATION OF DARKNESS

Each evening, shortly after sunset,
darkness covers the land.
    Having mystified thinkers for millennia,
    the mechanism for this occurrence
    has now been identified: migration.
Darkness, it has been found, is composed
of an almost infinite number of particles,
which roost and reproduce up north
where they have fewer natural enemies.
    Forest fires, lampposts, lasers, blazing sunlight,
    torches, candles, lighthouses, limelight, and electricity
    are relatively rare in the polar regions.
These lightweight bits of darkness
flock together and fly south each evening
to more fertile land in a never-ending search
for an abundant food supply.
With the coming of the rising sun,
they return to their northern nesting grounds.
However, not all specks of darkness migrate.
Some that are less adventurous
    or downright lazy
choose to stay behind.
These covey together, in varying numbers,
seeking shelter from the strong sunlight
    by gathering under leafy trees, behind
    large rocks, and underneath umbrellas;
    hiding in alleys, between parked cars,
    in caves, and inside empty pockets.
These clusters are perceived by us as shadows.
They have a somewhat shorter life span
than those which migrate.

THE MOON AND THE MOTH

The moth,
programmed by untold eons
    of evolution,
uses the moon as a beacon
to navigate its flight.

But how has the moon
fallen from the nighttime sky
and become attached
to this post on the porch?

This white-winged lunar explorer
using all the bug logic
    at her dutiful disposal
frantically orbits the porch light
    like a crazed Apollo astronaut
on an endless excursion to oblivion.

As a *deus ex machina* of sorts
in this little insect drama,
    I mercifully
Switch off the light.

Now free from the mesmerizing
    pull of the moon,
the moth breaks out of orbit
and flutters safely back to Earth.

On this flight
at least,
the fates flew with her.

THE NATURE OF A WEATHER NUT

At 11:45 in the morning
I hear the National Weather Service
issue a tornado warning
that advises all
to head to their basements.

I immediately
head to my back porch
with my camera.

THE NEW RANDOM DICTIONARY

In an effort to reflect accurately the inherent randomness of the universe we inhabit, the *New Random Dictionary of the English Language* lists more than 500,000 words, in no particular order, at least not alphabetical. "Alphabetizing words," the editor suggests in the preface (found on page 1,347), "is most definitely passé." Oftentimes, a correct definition follows an entry, but that cannot be helped. As the editor points out, "The laws of probability dictate against it." Spelling is usually accurate, but whether it is phonetic, obsolete, or the accepted variation of modern usage is anybody's guess. The pronunciation is given with an elaborate key that appears across the bottom of each facing page. However, the symbols are of absolutely no help in colloquial pronunciation, being those – according to the dictionary – of "guttural Babylonian used immediately prior to the construction of the Tower." For those interested in etymologies, they appear in square brackets following the definitions. Nevertheless, it seems the compilers of the illustrious undertaking did not place a major emphasis on this area of interest. Etymologies are often listed as "Of obscure origin" or "This one is a real puzzler!"; or in the majority of cases, "How are we supposed to know something as ridiculously archaic as this one?" It is hoped that there is a purpose to all this randomness. But to the casual reader, even with the help of advanced mathematical extrapolations and computer analyses, it should be shrugged off as beyond the scope of practical investigation and left to the domain of philosophers, and other visionaries.

THE NIGHT THE HEAVENS FELL

The night of the Perseid shower of shooting stars
we snuck out into the darkness minutes after midnight
    and gathered up as many of the fallen stars
as our greedy little hands could hold.

The yellow stars were the size of baseballs
    so we grabbed our gloves
and tried shagging them as they bounded out of the heavens.
Sure I made a few errors, but nobody was keeping score;
it was all in fun.

The red stars were as big as beachballs,
    and being bloated with gas,
floated rather than fell to earth.
We bounced them about until they either burst
or got caught on a high, out of reach, place.
We lost a couple in the cedar tree.

The miniature white stars
were too hot to touch even with a baseball mitt,
    so we let them drop to the ground.
Luckily, my father kept some golf clubs in the garage.
We used these to putt the little white balls
    into the black holes
we found scattered about the newly-mown lawn.
We couldn't miss sinking them.

The biggest challenge of the whole night
(if you don't count sneaking out of the house
    without waking my mom and dad)

was catching the comets, which were whizzing overhead,
    onto the end of a long stick.
Once hooked, they would spin around like sparkling pinwheels
    until their energy was spent;
the icy comets would plop to the ground
with slushy thuds.

We stored the comets in an ice cooler until we had enough
    (it took us almost until dawn).
Then we had the best snowball fight I can ever remember!
Maybe, because it was in August.

THE PUGILIST PHILOSOPHER

I never thought
much of Mike Tyson
until Roland told me,
Tyson once quipped,

"Everyone has a plan
until they get punched
in the face."

Now I rank him up there
with Marcus Aurelius.

THE RESULT OF THE DIG

"So it finally turned out that after endless years of digging and researching, the only bones found at the Olduvai Gorge were those of fellow anthropologists, who likewise were searching for earlier evolutionary specimens. You had Neanderthals looking for Homo Erectus, Homo Erectus excavating for Australopithecus, Australopithecus probing for the early anthropoid apes, who in turn sought out the first mammals. The earliest thing they found was a tree shrew, and nobody knows exactly what he might have been looking for, though frankly by that time nobody gave a damn."

THE ULTIMATE PARTY

All 117 billion people who once
inhabited the Earth are invited
to a party. The invitations state
8 p.m., and to my surprise give
my apartment as the place. The
dress is casual. They all arrive
within a couple of hours of each
other. But the party's a bomb.
There is very little food, no space,
and the various languages present
a communications problem. After
a while, tempers grow short and fights
break out. One in the kitchen is
unusually violent for a party and
a man is stabbed. He turns out to be
the first man. He dies. In turn
everyone else disappears in order
of birth, dating back almost three million
years. This takes some time, and goes
on well into the middle of the night.
Finally I am left alone with
117 billion cups and glasses to clean.
I put it off until morning.

THIS AIN'T NO BLUES SONG

I say to my pal Paul, an accomplished blues guitarist, while we walk our kids to school, "You hear that train in the distance, that means there's an east wind blowing today". It's early in the morning. Paul probably got home from a gig at The House Of Blues about 5 a.m. I can tell he really doesn't care about my meteorological observation, but I go on anyway. "Yea, it's probably a freight train." Now, that piques his interest. Sleepily he says, "Once when I was playing in Kansas City I saw a train with over 100 of those things. I think I counted 111." "That's cool", I say. But I wonder why a blues musician wouldn't know what those things are? I know that improvisation and unpredictability are fundamental to the Blues, but... "those things?"

If they had tests you had to pass to become a blues musician wouldn't that be question number one:

1) You grow up in the rural south. A steam engine chugs along the tracks outside the shack you call home. You look up while pickin' at your guitar, take a sip of moonshine, and count the number of things that the locomotive is pulling. What are those things called?

Anyway, by the time we got the kids to school we decided those things were... boxcars!

I don't know if Howling Wolf, Leadbelly or even Boxcar Willie would be proud of us, but at that time in the morning we felt like we scored one hell of a victory.

TICK TOCK

With an old-time
 grandfather clock
  you can not only
   see time fly by
     you can hear it.

TIME

The Zen of When

TO THE WITCH

I told her
she was
the most intelligent
creature on the planet.

Well,
except maybe for some dolphins.

She laughed
as she launched
herself into the air
squealing with such delight.

TO GRANDMA

Sooner or later
every poet
writes a poem
about his grandmother.

Not me.

I never
wrote a poem
about my grandmother.

TO GRANDMA #2

You can live on
in other people's consciousnesses
incubating as memories.
It is important to keep memories
of your relatives alive.
Right, Grandma?!

Ernestine Marcello (1886-1972)

WE MIGHT BE

We might be fully aware
of the first time we do something,
but we should also pay attention
to what might also be
the last time

to our every action in our lives.
It is common today to say
"be mindful."
I like this term.

A few years ago,
I said to my boys,
"I don't think
we are going camping
this summer."
And my younger son
Peter Paul said,

"Dad, we haven't camped
in over three years."

YOU THERE!

Biking home
in Cambridge
talking to
Roland
in my ear buds
a speeding car
brushed by me.
The last words
Roland heard
were, "That guy
is an asshole."

* * *

A-holes to the left
of me, A-holes to
the right of me.

* * *

So today at this
service for Pete,
I'll do his bidding.
Instead of the
traditional Kiss
of Peace, the
shaking of hands
of our neighbors,
let's go Jersey Style.

* * *

Point to those nearby
and demand: "Hey you
there. You an asshole?"

* * *

Amen.

AUTOBIOGRAPHY

I got
my first car
at 17.

www.ingramcontent.com/pod-product-compliance
Lightning Source LLC
Chambersburg PA
CBHW051659040426
42446CB00009B/1219